## MEASURING AND COMPARING

# How Big Is Big?
## Comparing Plants

### Vic Parker

Heinemann
LIBRARY

Chicago, Illinois

**www.heinemannraintree.com**
Visit our website to find out
more information about
Heinemann-Raintree books.

**To order:**

☎ Phone 888-454-2279

💻 Visit www.heinemannraintree.com
to browse our catalog and order online.

© 2011 Heinemann Library
an imprint of Capstone Global Library, LLC
Chicago, Illinois

Edited by Nancy Dickmann, Rebecca Rissman, and Sian Smith
Designed by Victoria Allen
Picture research by Hannah Taylor
Original illustrations © Capstone Global Library 2011
Original illustrations by Victoria Allen
Production by Victoria Fitzgerald
Originated by Dot Gradations Ltd
Printed in China

14 13 12
10 9 8 7 6 5 4 3

Library of Congress Cataloging-in-Publication Data
Parker, Victoria.
  How big is big?:comparing plants / Vic Parker.
      p. cm.—(Measuring and comparing)
  Includes bibliographical references and index.
  ISBN 978-1-4329-3959-5 (hc)—ISBN 978-1-4329-3967-
0 (pb) 1. Plant size—Juvenile literature. 2.  Weights and
measures—Juvenile literature.  I. Title.
  QK641.P325 2011
  530.8'1—dc22                    2010000932

## Acknowledgments

The author and publisher are grateful to the following for
permission to reproduce copyright material: Alamy Images
pp. 22 (© Cody Duncan), 24 (© Fabian Gonzales Editorial);
© Capstone Publishers pp. **5**, **7**, **8**, **9**, **26**, **27** (Karon Dubke);
FLPA p. **11** (John Eveson); istockphoto pp. **20 right**, **10**
(© Octavio Campos Salles), **16 left** (© Kyoungil Jeon);
Photolibrary pp. **6** (Tetra Images), **12 left** (Garden Picture
Library/Andrew Lord), **16 right** (David M. Dennis), **18**
(Kalhoefer Kelly); shutterstock pp. **4** (© FloridaStock),
**12 right** (© Vibrant Image Studio), **20 left** (© Elena Elisseeva);
www.artdirectors.co.uk p. **14** (Lawrence Reemer).

Photographs used to create silhouettes: shutterstock, cactus
(© Alegria), redwood (© Steven Bourelle), palm (© Viktoria),
daffodil (© AlexandraStock), sunflower (© Kudryashka).

Cover photograph of a group of sequoia trees called bachelor
and the three graces in Yosemite National Park (2008). Image
reproduced with permission of Alamy (© Astrid Harrisson).

Every effort has been made to contact copyright holders
of material reproduced in this book. Any omissions will
be rectified in subsequent printings if notice is given to
the publisher.

## Disclaimer

# Contents

Words appearing in the text in bold, **like this**,
are explained in the glossary.

# What Is Big?

When we use the word "big," we are talking about the size of something compared to something else. For example, a cruise ship is big compared to a motorboat.

A cruise ship is longer, taller, and wider than a motorboat.

It is not always easy to figure out which thing is the biggest. To decide if one thing is bigger than another, we often have to look at more than one measurement.

Is the carrot or the orange bigger? The carrot is longer, but the orange is wider.

# Height, Length, and Width

When we measure an object, we can look at its height, length, or width. The height of something is how tall it is. An object can be tall or short.

One type of dog can be taller than another.

height

The length of something is how long it is. An object can be long or short. The width of something is how far it is from side to side. An object can be wide or narrow.

An eggplant is wider than a green bean.

width

length

# Measuring Size

We measure something's **length**, **height**, and **width** to find out how big it is. We measure big sizes in feet (ft.) and smaller sizes in inches (in.).

The length of this cucumber is being measured in inches.

Different tools help us to measure length, height, and width. You can use a ruler, tape measure, or measuring stick.

A tape measure can measure longer things than a ruler can.

# Plants

Some plants are big, while others are small. Plants need sunlight to grow. By growing tall and spreading out wide, plants can get the sunlight they need, even in crowded **rain forests**.

In a rain forest, lots of plants grow in a small amount of space.

It takes some plants a long time to grow big. Huge oak trees grow very slowly. They do not reach their full size for about 60 years. They can live to be more than 400 years old.

An oak tree has a tall, thick trunk and long branches.

# How Long Is a Leaf?

Have you ever seen a spider plant? A spider plant's long, thin leaves can be 16 inches long. Spider plants come from Africa, but people from around the world now have them in their homes.

spider plant

coconut palm

A coconut palm is the tree that coconuts come from. Its leaves can be 13 feet long. It would take 10 spider plant leaves to be as long as a coconut palm leaf.

**Remember!**
12 in. = 1 ft.

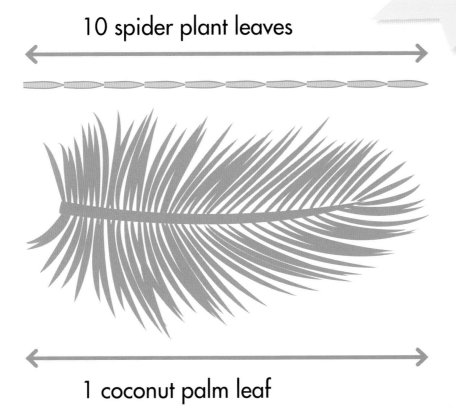

10 spider plant leaves

1 coconut palm leaf

**What is longer than a coconut palm leaf?** ➡

# Palm Leaves

An Amazonian bamboo palm leaf is longer than a coconut palm leaf. Amazonian bamboo palms live in warm **climates**. Their leaves are some of the longest in the plant world.

The bamboo palm tree's long leaves can be used to make hats, shoes, and rope.

The bamboo palm's leaves can be an amazing 66 feet long! It would take over five coconut palm leaves, laid end to end, to be as long as a bamboo palm leaf.

5 coconut palm leaves

1 Amazonian bamboo palm leaf

**A bamboo palm leaf is long and big. What else is big?** ➡

# How Wide Is a Water Lily?

Water lilies grow in ponds. Their **roots** anchor them to the bottom, and their wide leaves float on the surface. The leaves of garden pond water lilies can measure 12 inches wide.

water lily

titan arum flower

The titan arum **flower** is the biggest flower in the world. A titan arum flower can be over 3 feet wide. This is wider than three water lilies laid side by side.

3 water lilies

1 titan arum flower

**What is wider than a titan arum flower?** ➡

# Giant Leaves

Giant Amazonian water lilies have leaves much wider than a titan arum **flower**. These plants live in waters near the Amazon River in South America.

A giant Amazonian water lily could hold the weight of a one-year-old child!

A giant Amazonian water lily leaf can grow to around 6½ feet wide. It would take two titan arum flowers to be as wide as this.

2 titan arum flowers

1 giant Amazonian water lily

**A water lily is wide and big. What else is big?** ➡

# How Tall Is a Flower?

Many plants grow tall so that they can reach above other plants and take in more sunlight. Daffodils are often seen in spring. Some daffodils are about 18 inches tall.

sunflower

daffodil

A sunflower is taller than a daffodil. Some types of sunflowers grow to be about 10 feet tall. Six daffodils on top of each other would still be shorter than a sunflower.

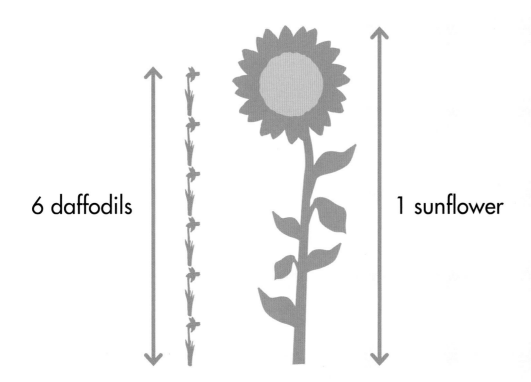

6 daffodils                                1 sunflower

**What is taller than a sunflower?** ➡

# Giant Cactuses

Cactuses can be even taller than sunflowers. Cardón cactuses grow in hot, dry **deserts**. They are some of the tallest cactuses in the world.

Cactuses can live in deserts because they store water in their thick **stems**.

A Cardón cactus can grow to be over 62 feet tall. This is even taller than six sunflowers on top of each other.

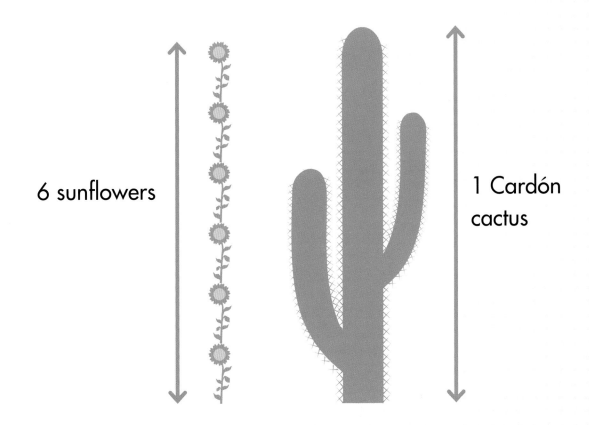

6 sunflowers

1 Cardón cactus

**What is taller than a cactus?** ➡

# Coast Redwoods

Some trees are taller than a Cardón **cactus**.
Trees are tall plants with woody **stems**. Coast
redwoods grow in mountain forests. They
are the tallest trees in the world.

Coast redwoods
can live for more
than 2,000 years.

The tallest coast redwood tree is more than 377 feet tall. You would need just over six Cardón cactuses on top of each other to be as tall as this coast redwood.

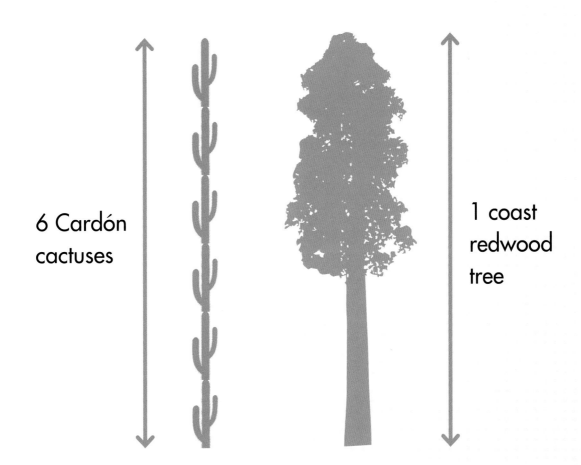

6 Cardón cactuses

1 coast redwood tree

# Measuring Activity

**Things you will need:** some leaves of different shapes and sizes, a ruler or tape measure, a pencil, and paper.

(1) Look carefully at your leaves. Which one do you think is the biggest?

(2) Measure the **length** of each leaf, and write down the results.

(3) Measure the **width** of each leaf, and write down the results.

**Find out:** Which leaf is the longest? Which leaf is the widest? Do you think you were right about which leaf is the biggest?

# Size Quiz and Facts

Units for measuring height, length, and width

Small sizes are measured in inches (in.).

Big sizes are measured in feet (ft.).

## Quiz

1. What unit would you use to measure the **height** of a tree?

   a) inches   b) feet

2. What unit would you use to measure the **width** of the trunk of a small tree?

   a) inches   b) feet

3. What unit would you use to measure the **length** of a carrot?

   a) inches   b) feet

Answers: 1 = b   2 = a   3 = a

## Big Plant Facts

- The longest carrot ever recorded measured over 19 feet long.

- A type of seaweed called Pacific giant kelp has the longest fronds (leaf-like parts) of any plant. Each frond can grow to almost 200 feet long.

- The world's widest living plant is a Montezuma cypress tree, in the state of Oaxaca in Mexico. In 2005 it was measured to be more than 36 feet wide.

- The world's tallest tree is a redwood that people have named Hyperion. It grows in a national park in California. It is over 377 feet high.

# Glossary

**cactus**  type of plant that mainly grows in deserts and dry places. Cactuses are often prickly.

**climate**  usual kind of weather in a place

**desert**  dry area of land where it does not rain much. Not many plants will grow in deserts because the land is so dry.

**flower**  part of a plant that makes seeds

**height**  how tall or high something is

**length**  how long something is

**rain forest**  type of forest that grows in a hot place where it often rains. Rain forests are usually crowded with lots of plants and trees that stay green all year round.

**root**  part of a plant that holds it in the ground. Roots bring water to the plant.

**stem**  part of a plant that holds it up. Stems also carry water to different parts of the plant.

**width**  how wide something is or how much it measures from side to side

# Find Out More

## Books

Barraclough, Sue. *Investigate: Plants*. Chicago: Heinemann Library, 2009.

Ganeri, Anita. *From Seed to Sunflower (How Living Things Grow series)*. Chicago: Heinemann Library, 2006.

Hewitt, Sally. *How Big Is It? (Measuring series)* North Mankato, MN: Stargazer, 2008.

## Web Sites

**www.mbgnet.net/bioplants/adapt.html**
On this website you can find out about interesting plants that live in different habitats.

**www.funbrain.com/measure/**
Try this simple quiz, which asks you to identify the correct measurements in inches.

# Index